BOOK SEVENTEEN

Also by Greg Delanty

POETRY COLLECTIONS

Cast in the Fire

Southward

American Wake

The Hellbox

The Blind Stitch

The Ship of Birth

Collected Poems, 1986–2006

The New Citizen Army

Loosestrife

SPECIAL POETRY EDITIONS

The Fifth Province

Striped Ink

TRANSLATIONS

Selected Poems of Kyriakos Charalambides

Selected Poems of Seán Ó Ríordáin

EDITED ANTHOLOGIES

Jumping Off Shadows: Selected Contemporary Irish Poets
(with Nuala Ní Dhomhnaill)

New and Selected Poems of Patrick Galvin
(with Robert Welch)

The Word Exchange: Anglo-Saxon Poems in Translation
(with Michael Matto)

BOOK SEVENTEEN

POEMS

Greg Delanty

LOUISIANA STATE UNIVERSITY PRESS
BATON ROUGE

Published by Louisiana State University Press
Copyright © 2015 by Greg Delanty
All rights reserved
Manufactured in the United States of America
LSU Press Paperback Original
First printing

Designer: Laura Roubique Gleason
Typeface: Minion Pro
Printer and binder: Lightning Source

LIBRARY OF CONGRESS CATALOGING-IN-PUBLICATION DATA
Delanty, Greg, 1958–
  [Poems. Selections]
  Book seventeen : poems / Greg Delanty.
    pages ; cm
  ISBN 978-0-8071-5970-5 (softcover : acid-free paper) —
ISBN 978-0-8071-5971-2 (epub) — ISBN 978-0-8071-5972-9 (pdf)
— ISBN 978-0-8071-5973-6 (mobi)
  I. Title.
  PR6054.E397A6 2015
  821'.914—dc23
                            2014033787

The paper in this book meets the guidelines for permanence and durability of the Committee on Production Guidelines for Book Longevity of the Council on Library Resources. ∞

γυνή τις—λέγοις ἂν ἀτρύφερον—παραστείχει
    ἡμέτερον δόμον. ἄρτι ἐγερθεὶς ἀγανακτικῶς εἶχον·
ἡ δὲ γαληνῶς μειδήσασα σῖγα
    λέγει· "ἴδου τὴν αὔγην ἡλίου ἐν λίμνῃ·
ἴδου κλύμενον ζωπυρούμενον ῥοδοδάκτυλον
    ξανθῷ πυρί· ὁδοιπόρων ἐν Ὁδῷ Βορείῳ ἅπαξ ἡσυχάζων,
ἀκούειν ἔξεστι ξουθοπτέρου πτέρυγας
    στρεφόμενας μετεώρου." ὀρθρίᾳ ἄλλῃ γαλήνη τόση
μ' ἠνώχλησε ἄν· ἀλλὰ ὡς ἄπλαστος
    ὁ τρόπος. αὐτὴν λάνθανω.
ἀφωπλισμένος δὲ ἀφίημι ταῦτα οἷς ἀγανακτῶ
    καὶ ἐπεὶ οὐδεὶς θεὸς συμφέρεται
λογίζομααι—οἱ ἄλλοι θεοὶ ἄπαντες ὄξος—ὅτι
    δεῖ νέον κόσμον ποιεῖν καὶ αὐτὴν ὀνομάζεειν
Ἡσυχίαν ἢ Ἀτρεμῆν καὶ ἀναβιβάζειν Ἀλκυόνα
    καὶ κελεύειν Ἀφροδίτην,
Ἄρην, Ἄρτέμιδα, καὶ Δία αὐτόν, χώρειν μὲν γυναῖκι ταύτῃ,
    ἐν μέσῳ δὲ καταστῆναι, ἢ κούφως παρέρχεται
ἡμέτερον δόμον ὀρθρίᾳ ταύτῃ ἀμβροσίᾳ.

                              —Nikos Metapheron

Where now is the memory of those days
that were yours on earth, their joys
and sorrows, making a universe of your own?

    —Jorge Luis Borges, "To a Minor Poet of the Greek Anthology"
    (translated by Greg Delanty)

CONTENTS

Preface   xvii

[*A frequent query about* The Greek Anthology *is why many poets have Latinate names. The Romans considered Greek to be superior to Latin, and the language of culture, and therefore they wrote in Greek, but kept their Latin names.*]

GRIGOROGRAPHOS
The First Story   1
Free Flow   1

MARIA THE MYTHOLOGIST
Recycling   2

GREGORY OF CORKUS
Below the Monument of Lysicrates   2
Fall Out   3
Party Piece   3
A Special Bond   4
Company   4

DEANOS THE BEARDED
Hey You   5

FRANKOS KAVALARIS
Reflection   5

ROVIUS FLACCUS
Rock Bottom   6
The God of Slights   6

PLUVIUS
Appreciation 7
Whiteout 7

IANIA THE SEER
Ye of Little Faith 8

GERYON MORFI
Bodysurfers 8

FERRIUS
The Immortalists 9

MARIS OF THE WEST
Race 9

MAKANNUS
The Fallacy Pathetic 10

DOGUS
Deities 10
Gaia's Inn 11
Driving in Vermont 12

ENDASI
Lapse 13

MACUDES OF LANT
In This Life 13

DAN THE YOUNGER
Paradise 14

PATTIA
Inklings 14

MOSIUS THE ASTRONOMER
The Event Horizon 15
Above the East River 15
Imagine 16

CLIONA OF LUTETIA
Market Morning 16

PATRIKIOS
The Lesson   17

LONGLIUS
Road Workers   17

MONTAGUS
Prelapsarian   18

IOANNIS PICTORIS
Chronicle   18

NIALLOS THE TEACHER
The Music of the Spheres   19

TERENCE OF THE NORTH
To a Teacher   19

NORMANIOS THE PHYSICIAN
Teenagers   20
Terminal   20

ROSANNA DAEDALUS
In a Diner above the Lamoille River   21

HONESTMEDON
Childhood   21
No Man's Land   22
Eventually   22
A New Law   23

MUNDUS MUNATIUS THE MODERN
At the Bar in The Daily Planet   23

JONOUALES PROTECTOR
The New Opiate   24

CLARA KRITIKOS
After Listening to the World News Again   24

ALIKI OF OLIVES
Entering the Acropolis   25

MARCES THE DIDACT
Coat of Arms 25

MAKIBBENUS
Ostraka 26

DANICHORUS
New Ostia 26
Another Empire 27
Odysseus 27
Father Abroad 28
Life 28
Parents 29

FRANCES THE PRIESTESS
Go-Between 29

NUALLIA
The Divorced Mother 30

ANTONIUS THE ELDER
Humilities 30

HEANIUS
Goddess of the Hearth 31
Concealment 31

GRADIUS
The Old Country 32

SIRRIOS
The Green Line 32

ELENI OF THE MESSENGER
Resort 33

ANTIPATER THE TRAVELLER
Foreigner 33
The Mechanic 34
Heat Wave in Sitia 34

CHRISTOPHER SILENTIARIUS
The Third Voyage 35

LIAMOS OF THE SOUTH
Templenoe   35

KINCELLAS MAJOR
Weather Relief   36

GIORGIOS OF AKOVOS
Good Company   36
The Wall   37

SIMEON THE SECOND
Sermon   38

DAVIDUS MELBURNIUS
The Apostle in Corinth   39

DEREKUS OF THE ISLANDS
Visiting the Church of Saint John of the Apocalypse, Patmos   39

HIRSCHION
Sleep   40

PHIONA
Our Times   40

EAMONNUS
Dawn   41
Birth Notice   41

ELIZÁVETH GRAMMATICA
Breakfast   42

JOHN THE MAKER
The Poetry World   42
Lulu's Family Diner   43
To a Poet Friend   43
The Small Picture   44

ARION
Dropping Names   44

DAVIDOS BARBAROS
Arion's Retribution   45

IUDITH THE EDITOR
To Those in the Shade   46

TOBINGRAPHOS
The Era of Busy   46
Master Tardy   47

GRENNANUS
"The Good Die Young"   47

THOMAS THE GARDENER
Understory   48

ANTONEL OF CARRACIUS
About Time   48

IOUDITH EIKONOPLASTIS
Special Days   49

REIDUS PROTOMASTORAS
In Praise of Failure   49

A Selection from the Athenian Workshop Papyrus   50

DANDIUS
I. Aubade   50

ANONYMOUS (probably the young RAKIUS)
II. PASU   50

COFFIUS
III. Cycles   51

COLMOS GAELICUS
IV. The Artist's Disgrace   51

ALLOFUS
The Most Neglected God of All   52

RAKIUS
The Ladykiller   53
The Goat   53
Tug-of-War   54
Addict   54
On Miami Beach   55

ANONYMOUS
Escaping the Party   55

HEPHAESTUS OF ATHENS
From the Acropolis View Hotel   56
Return   56

MEDANES
"Try Again, Dolt"   57
Mercy   57

TRICIA ARGENTIA
Purgatory   58

HARVUS
Payment   58

GREGOR
Avaunt   59

LANIUS
The Rat   59
"It's an Ill Wind That Blows No Good"   60
The Break-up Contract   60
Meeting Again   61
Later   61

ALANOS
Old Flame   62

KATERINA PHILIA
A Quiet Glory   62

THE WATCHMAN OF SPARTA
Worth Remembering   63

GALIA OF ITHAKI
The Caryatids in the Acropolis   63

EVANTHOULA
The New Athena   64

DAVUS THE CONSUL
Laughter   65

NIKOS METAPHERON
Disarming   66

GALI METAPHRASTRIA
Patient   67

JAIUS
Speaking Plainly   67

ARAN OF THE ARCHIPELAGO
Fathoming   68
Well You Know This Fish   68

BENOS
The New Pastoralists   69

PANOS KINNELLUS
The Other   69
The Winner   70

RICARDUS LAMBUS
Old-Timers   70

HARTNETTON
Life   71

BERNARDIOS SCHOLASTICUS
Another Time   71
Wonder of Wonders   72

BILLIUS THE LAUREATE
News in Flight   72

STRATO OF ATHENS
Time Travel   73

GREGORIS PERIPLANÓMENOS
The Traveler's Grace   73

Dedications and Acknowledgments   75

PREFACE

Book Seventeen is a contemporary book, giving a sense of the times. It adds to the sixteen books of the original *Greek Anthology*, which is made up of short poems ranging over a thousand years, beginning from the seventh century BC. The poems include a wide range of epigrams, which may be described variously as amatory, religious, dedicatory, sepulchral, hortatory, declamatory, and satirical. The earliest known anthology in Greek was compiled in the first century BC by Meleager under the title *Anthologia*, or "Garland." In his preface, Meleager describes his arrangement of the poems as a garland of flowers woven together. Thus the word *anthology* came to mean a collection of literary works. *Book Seventeen* extends this tradition by garlanding voices of my own creation.

The arrangement of the poems is by the poets' names. The poem in Greek at the beginning appears as "Disarming" later in the volume. There will be a Book Eighteen, though this book may be better served by having other poets' work, and maybe this will continue even to later books.

Many of these poems have been published over the past decade, going back to issue 157 of *PN Review* (2003), where twenty-two of them first appeared along with a version of this preface. A number of the poems have also been published under my own name, and will appear in future anthologies in this way with the author's blessing.

BOOK SEVENTEEN

The First Story

The email, telling a friend *we're not too bad considering*
       the state of the world, crosses the Atlantic
with the touch of a key. The leaves of an evergreen blow
       like a shoal of emerald fish returning to the same place.
A cardinal in his scarlet robes pecks the feeder.
       The bells of the Angelus ring from St. Joseph's,
the Angel of the Lord declares unto Mary. The infant god
       of my childhood is back on earth again, the one
I've ceased to believe in, the lifebelt that keeps believers afloat
       in the storm of being here, issuing tickets
to the hereafter ever since that episode in the garden,
       the tall tale of our banishment concocted by some storyteller
who'd be so flummoxed we've taken it for gospel
       he'd simply say: "Look around you now. Behold, the garden."

Free Flow

The waterfall bathes "the feet of Mount Parnassus,"
       which is how a local described these lower slopes
in the town of Delphi, calling to mind Jesus
       washing the feet of his disciples before he
turned bread and wine into the body
       and blood of God. This is no blasphemy.
The gods flow freely in and out of each other.

Recycling

If myths are frameworks, then any one person's story
      is made from a scrap heap: a Cyclops here,
Chimera there, Asclepius one minute, Persephone the next.
      Each is like a bicycle put together from old parts:
a rusty chain, racer handlebars, mudguards, an odd tire.
      When people see you their eyes say *what a hybrid,*
how weird, how cool, how funny,
      awesome. They laugh. It may even have a rusty bell
or horn to warn everyone, "Get out of the way, pronto."
      Still it gets you where you're going. The wheels turn.

Below the Monument of Lysicrates

My son shouts up to our balcony from the Road of the Tripods
      that he's got a new flute, fingers a tune.
Gods and godlings perk up their ears: the terracotta pantheon
      displayed in tourist shop windows, the broken busts
around the Acropolis—Silenus shouldering the stage of Dionysus
      within sight of our window, Molpos, Apollo, Athena on high.
Once again the victory of the choral festival
      is lifted on this ancient road.

Fall Out

Today I read a poet's elegy for his friend
      written forty years after he passed away.
It hurt me to read, how friendship still shone,
      a paradigm of friendlove, the jewel
in the crown of life. And I thought of you,
      and wished I was that poet, and you had died
in the good old days, and it was I wrote that poem
      to you, my friend, my sometime friend.

Party Piece

Often the get-together is unavoidable:
      a marriage, funeral, function.
You brace yourself, most people being more
      friendly acquaintances than acquainted friends
—even with the latter you feel more at ease meeting one
      at a time, tuning into each other's frequency.
You tire of shop talk, gossip, sport-babble,
      politics, nervy jokes you laugh at too soon.
Tell yourself not to drink too much or your party mask
      will slip as you balance on the social pergola,
or rather the unsteady plinth of society, the necessary base.

A Special Bond

Funny, heartening, to live for years in a town
        and know simply by sight this face or that,
to maybe nod the vaguest of hellos on a crowded street.
        Neither ever crosses the line,
the border into intimacy, freed
        from claustrophobic ties
fraught with squabbles, slights, rivalry,
        the regular pressure of close relations.
One feels a peculiar fondness for them. Whatever
        you do, don't attempt to chat, become friendly.
Stifle any such urge at bus queue or shop counter.
        Perilous it would be to risk shattering such
a special bond, this remote intimacy.

Company

A secluded table in a café affords me a modicum
        of privacy. I settle down to read, work
among clusters talking sport, politics, shop,
        whiling away time. It's easy to feel warmth,
love even, towards others from this vantage.
        My jacket reserves the nearest chair
for my imminent friend, putting anybody off
        sitting too close, starting up conversation.
My company has arrived, Solitude herself.

Hey You

   If you could observe a cheerful friend, loving father,
serene sister by themselves, it would be like scrutinizing a face
   as the person descends from Holy Communion,
or stands alone over a family grave; all the stranger
   for being familiar. Each countenance as disconcerting
as when you catch yourself in a mirror,
   though by then you're aware—
if you could look without forethought
   you'd wonder who that person is,
how sad, glum, odd that face.

Reflection

We think too much of what people think, the shadows
   they cast that we see as our own,
imagined or true. Horses galloping the beach
   aren't bothered by their dark reflections on wet sand.
They don't need shadow-blinds like highly strung thoroughbreds
   for fear their adumbrations will scare them.
Let's forget the umbras cast by ourselves and others.
   Let's drop the shadow-blinds.

Rock Bottom

The god of life brings us down with a look,
      a comment, and we hit rock bottom. It could be worse.
From below you can make out skate hovering like hawks
      in the heavens, the anemone swaying
in the zephyr currents, the angler-fish casting his ignis fatuus bait
      from his forehead to trick innocents
into his diabolic mouth, the great silhouetted shoals
      flying like arrows shot from the bow of Poseidon
—the gods still fighting ancient battles beneath the surface.
      I am a crusty old lobster safe in my crevice,
brandishing a boxing glove claw, jabbing at all
      who venture near. God of life, leave me here.

The God of Slights

The list of cuts that the sly god of slights
      entices people to inflict is endless: "You're always late";
"You live in the lah-di-dah section of town rather
      than the hoi polloi side"; "You tip parsimoniously."
Slight slights often tone-shot behind the shield
      of a joke. Each like a splinter in the foot
that you ignore, thinking nothing of the prick
      at first. As the day wears on
you curse, hobble about looking for a needle to pry it
      from the inflamed skin, the seed watered
by the niggling vexation that it's got so embedded.
      You swear next time you'll not
forget to tread softly, not forget to wear slippers.

Appreciation

We curse the drizzle, downpour, hailstone, torrent,
    the cats and dogs, the deluge that clears the air
accompanied by Lightning and his laggard brother, Thunder.
    Maybe such insults are too much for the god
and he throws a tantrum, catches us without an umbrella
    at a football game or picnic, no shelter in sight.
But this god is soft by nature; without him
    we'd be minus the multitudinous shades
of green, the harvests of Demeter, the gifts, bounty he showers
    on all. Bow down now to the god of precipitation,
this brooding cumulus god, this weeping god of the sky.

Whiteout

The day gets away from me. Nothing done
    and it's lunchtime, rushing to a meeting,
held up by whiteout traffic, the snow
    calling a halt to the daily life-and-death tedium:
committees, bills, email, post. If we croaked today
    what difference would it make? I give up,
tell myself to wait till the traffic eases off.
    Park. Drop into a shop. Watch the snow
erase the world. It is good to throw
    your hat at it all, not to turn up, be nothing, no one,
watch the snow fall, turn to a blank page.

Ye of Little Faith

People walk, slide, glide, hula-hoop,
       somersault and land again
making their mark, signatures, circles
       within circles, brief squiggles, doodles on the surface.
Some laugh, some are deadly serious: children, mothers,
       fathers, lovers, friends, loners. People fall,
get up again, and not just on the frozen lake
       beyond our window. Daily you walk
on water yourself. Have faith.

Bodysurfers

Nothing like it, to catch a ride on the comber,
       the muscle of the breaker curls into a wing,
Hermes' strained scapula. We bodysurf the ruffled feathering
       of the water's wonder,
both messenger and message in the pinioned thunder.

The Immortalists

Youngsters climb the gorge, limber as goats, leap thirty feet
    into a pool no more than two yards wide
surrounded by sharp limestone outcrops.
    There's no room for error. I watch these high flyers
from the precipice opposite. I can't bear to look down,
    want to holler *Stop,* but know that kids don't listen.
Besides, should one diver take notice he might hesitate,
    a glimmer of fear his downfall.
For now they're immortal, the temporary immortalists.

Race

We lounge under the shade of an ash
    in a hotel compound on Lake Morey.
The slobbering water laps the shore like a dog
    licks its master, spittle-scum dripping.
The lake floor is mushy, a slime of sand
    with strands of green weed.
The wetsuit children play games, frolic,
    screech from boats or diving boards.
Their lives are concerned with nothing now
    but sport. They run the three-legged race,
strapped at the ankle to their privileged lives.

The Fallacy Pathetic

There's something confused about the wind today,
    demented, unruly,
the bushes and trees not knowing which way
    to turn—a bit like yours truly.
That's such an easy schoolbook analogy;
    pathetic fallacy, projection, codology.
The wind is nothing but its own alien element,
    and besides, to someone else it might be clement.

Deities

Like light from a star back of the universe
our multiverse voice reaches you as you kneel
in the mosque, church, synagogue, temple of your selves.
DanaUranusYahwehJesuVoidus—you name us.
We are legion, as many as there are stars
in the firmament, many extinct, many still to emerge.
Our voice is a heliograph saying we want to stay,
do not destroy us, we are the light
shining from the deep space within your atoms,
traveling so far, shape and shade changing
according to your terrain and lives. You've seen no less
in creatures: the leaf insect, the gecko,
the cocooning butterfly. We survive
as best we can in your diverse habitats.

Gaia's Inn

The owner informs us the inn's closed, summer's over,
    but we're welcome to a few beers, to sit on the deck.
We're sensible enough not to take any notice
    of the begging dog with a stick in his mouth.
Ignore him long enough and he'll give up
    just as the nagging mutt of weekday routine,
nitty-gritty responsibility, has let us be.
    Buoys tilt like planets, each with its own biosphere
of creatures and plants. Suds at the water's edge.
    It seems Gaia has washed her hands
of the motor boat, the jet stream harming her, the radio
    reporting the all-too-human news of the planet
heating up, that the only species which destroys
    its own habitat, is also the only one which creates gods.
The goddess reflects, "Ah, they've been at this deity-making forever,
    making something of themselves, *Homo Importanticus*.
Let's cut them slack. Soon enough there'll be no one here.
    Then where will we be without them?"

Driving in Vermont

The mountains are plumes of leaf-fire
      that people travel thousands of miles to admire.
Few spot the god making light of the trees, on vacation.
      No one asks him to dish out prophecy here.
Perhaps they're too afraid to find out what lies ahead.
      I bet he came on the urging of an Abnaki deity
in the egalitarian realm of the gods.
      Folk drive by, their radios reporting
the weather, last night's frost, baseball, the demise of the world
      in the umpteen ways we've devised. Maybe a few comment
on the glorious light, everyone hightailing it to work. But now
      my job is to pull off Route 15 at Hyde Park and Centerville
and report this sighting. Who'd have thought the god
      of light would be seen in the Northeast Kingdom,
Apollo himself, on the lam from his Attic stomping ground.

Lapse

We say our fate is in the lap of the gods, pray
    to our special deity, but the pantheon today
        stood up in dismay
            seeing us run out of control across the map.
The majority of them take flight
    to planets
        of distant galaxies whose denizens allow them to sit about.
The bushed gods who stick around stretch themselves out,
    take a millennial nap,
but not before they cast bets
    on whether Gaia, who is so sickly that she is laid out,
        will make it or not.
        Not a godly lap in sight.

In This Life

All certainty of eternity is out
    the door: Purgatory, Hell, Tartarus,
Heaven, Elysium, but now we doubt
    the certainty of such certainty also,
reaffirming the zonulet at the edge of Oceanus,
    the fog-shrouded Cimmerian land, or of Limbo,
the only uncertain states we'll certainly ever know.

Paradise

To be inside on a wet day, rain on the roof,
        the heavens opening, the diamond drops draping
the window. Nothing to do but hunker in, snug
        under the quilt, in the armchair
by the fire with a book, or watch a game,
        no pressure to cut the grass, oil the bike,
clean the car, run to the bank, jog, swim—
        freed from the taskmaster of good weather.

Inklings

Our 'un can't grasp the notion of size, convinced he can
        climb inside a toy bus, fit a football through a keyhole
—a regular phenomenon among toddlers. I fancy
        the child unconsciously recalls that first place
we're rumored to hail from, an Un
        -place where size means no thing, where we're more
like squid, size and shape changing, before our souls enter,
        settle in corporeal cells. And in this sentence
of flesh, inklings of our squidsouls leave us for dead
        in the ink cloud, having vamoosed back,
off, away, beyond into the lost Universe of Unsize.

The Event Horizon

Perhaps those zones where our souls are said to end up
        are possible: that region the good inhabit,
the zone where the imperfect are burnished perfect, the infernal place
        of no-hopers. The afterlife is no more unbelievable
than us landed here on this giant spinning-top
        whirling crookedly through space,

especially now the brains proclaim zones
        where time's altered, kaput; dimensions where stars slip
through self-generated cracks in space and so much more
        not dreamed of in our reality. Truly, after all,
the soul may have somewhere to go beyond the only event horizon
        we know of, our point of no return. Unbelievable.

Above the East River

The suspension bridge is a great hammock.
        If we could see other dimensions
we'd behold the god of ingenuity, Hephaestus,
        swinging ever so gently, slumbering above the traffic.

Imagine

We raise three inches of cordless chromium
        and natter with someone across the world
in another time zone. We've long outdone
        the gods, even Hephaestus with his robots,
his sundry inventions. Picture someone long dead,
        brought back from the underworld,
flummoxed, taking in the whole show.

Market Morning

Mouffetard, surely a street straight out of paradise,
        Heaven, Elysium, those myth spheres
I don't believe exist except upon earth. So, this
        is it, the ancient thoroughfare
between Lutetia and Rome, on a Saturday morning.
        Especially now Helios is out shopping
with everyone else. Fingers check pears,
        pick up ruby-red wine, gold bars of bread, bronze pies,
jade olives, amethyst grapes. Such a bonanza. Us lounging,
        blowing on frothy bowls of piping café au lait.

The Lesson

It's as if the god of unhappiness, of low-level discontent at least,
    injected his serum into our veins when born, inoculating us
from feeling good for long. He's like a grim schoolmaster
    patrolling the playground, reminding children
they've only a minute or two before the line-up bell,
    darkening unconscious happiness, marring natural mirth
with back-burner anxiety, fretful they'll have to line up soon
    and march back into interminable lessons, tests,
right and wrong answers, punishment, the classroom's dolor,
    learning by rote, the slow tick of the metronome,
the weight of responsibility; that life isn't *all* play.

Road Workers

I only noticed them, and then almost too late,
    —as we drove on, cursing the minor holdup—
the laborers as they perspired in orange jackets,
    pouring tar, working dinosaur diggers,
one with an insect-eater snout. Maybe it was Maria Callas
    on the radio that opened up the sacred,
brought me to my senses, the high way of art.
    There they were, the Lares of motorways,
laboring away, laying out ink-black tarmac
    in boiling sun. Sweating for us beneath hard hats.

Prelapsarian

The satyrs of the cottonwood trees spurt,
    shoot seed into the air all over the city
without embarrassment, or being branded indecent.
    How lucky they are, how un-self-conscious
these swingers of plants, these exhibitionists.
    Another tree before the Fall.

Chronicle

Bells ring all across Sunday morning.
    People are summoned to their gods.
Even to a nonbeliever the bells
    are sacred; the peal, the carillon,
the pistillate chimes of swaying metal flowers.
    The bells toll, loll soothing
as a foghorn, train whistle in the distance,
    hoot of a ship sailing into harbor.
Such sounds chime our sole divinity,
    intimations of humanity.

The Music of the Spheres

Eris visits us in different guises everyday.
She comes now via the tyranny of Muzak
everywhere we go: the mall, bus, street, café;
rock, reggae, rap, jazzack. For earth's sake,
drowning out the sound of nothing. Everyone fears
the sirens singing the silent music of the spheres.

To a Teacher

Once more you stand before a cabal of ephebi,
instructing them how to look at the sun.
You pin-hole a sheet of paper.
The light is blacked out, then emerges
out of the night of the moon.
                        Some pupils observe,
lit by learning, others show
not a glimmer of interest. How
can you guide them away
from eclipsing Acedia, Confusion,
Mammon: the dark gods of our day?
You bow your head as if before a shrine
reaching to set a candle alight.

Teenagers

They loiter, smoke, giggle, strut, wolf-whistle,
      shout obscene remarks, text, ogle
each other's crushes, torpedo into the Aegean.
      We hadn't heard school was out today,
curse these adultlets bursting with hormones,
      embarrassing to see as their acned faces,
their bodies sprouting hair. Don't be too
      hard on them. They're in
the cocoon agony, miserable, mortifying,
      alone. Ignoble to recall
even in old age. We should be kind,
      kindest of all to these. Spare them.

Terminal

And so, Tithonus, you're hooked
      to ventilator, catheter, or cannula,
gagging down another pill, unable to fend for yourself.
      You pray to be released from the drip
as malignant cells metastasize,
      make nothing of you. Dawn even
abandons you in the snug-as-a-coffin terminal room.
      Nurses turn you, change your diaper.
You're unable to recall your own name,
      remember you can't remember;
eternally aware dementia erases the spool.
      The gods, as usual, show no mercy.

In a Diner above the Lamoille River

The rocks below on the river trail foam fins
    as if they swim upstream along with the salmon
returning to spawning grounds, leaping falls, freshets,
    whirlpools, the ancient anonymous struggle.
The fish age instantly to mottled old-timers,
    dying in the nursing pools of their birth waters.
A tour group of elderly are the only other diners,
    their skin mottled not unlike the salmon.
They seem to get along. They jaw about the weather,
    the water height, the amount to tip.
One woman's shaky hand fills the patron questionnaire
    with praise. I scribble this on the back of mine,
and tip the kind waitress a little more than usual.
    She laid steaming bowls before them, a priestess
setting her libations on the altar of trembling elder gods.

Childhood

You wax lyrical about childhood being idyllic,
    a country under a spell:
a beach ball in the air, an uncle with the trick
    of a penny up his sleeve, a lick
of ice cream, blithe waving from the horses of a carousel
    galloping the hills of childhood. Well,
okay, but look again. The impaled horses circle.
    Their faces suggest they're being whipped through hell.

No Man's Land

Each dawn we struggle over the top
      of a regular day,
stumble on the barbed wire,
      the strewn bodies. Who'll cop
it this time? A brother? Friend?
      The bodies drop on all sides,
battling to the bunker of the next day.
      Our nerves so frayed
we begin to wish for our own end.

Eventually

In memory, Ton Koimismenon

The pot of grief,
all that is left of you,
bubbling on the blue flower
of a slow flame,

left there evaporating,
slipping the mind,
the water
all
but boiled
off.

A New Law

Let there be a ban on every holiday.
        No ringing in the new year.
No fireworks doodling the warm night air.
        No holly on the door. I say
let there be no more.
        For many are not here who were here before.

At the Bar in The Daily Planet

The gods are always at it, pick on each other,
Hera and Poseidon, Hades and Demeter; more human
than the humans themselves, or at least
that's the way it seemed, till today it struck me
as the barman jabbed at a regular with a barbed remark
and turned up the news, everyone glued to the latest Iliad:
it is humans who put the gods in the shade,
being such expert backstabbers, naysayers, killers.
Too late even for a *populus ex machina* to save the day.

The New Opiate

Such skill with a ball, club, missile in the air.
Each side prays to their god to annihilate
the opposition; to slaughter them, fair
or unfair, with something close to hate.
The players replace the deities who are dead.
The crowd's roar deafens. The gods go head to head.

After Listening to the World News Again

So, these days one is dimly consoled with the thought
Hell, even the sun will eventually come to naught.

Entering the Acropolis

In the temple of Athena Nike, the goddess smiles smugly
       down on the daily tourists in their comfortable Nikes.
She's won again. Not all victory is a matter of war. Complicity
       is the deity hardly anyone sees.

Coat of Arms

The two swordfish in the market are gawked at by all
       who pass. Parents coax wide-eyed children up to ogle.
One grinning family has a photograph taken alongside.
       Picture these noble knights of the sea being caught,
their bodies, great muscles, writhing on the deck.
       The fish could be the heraldic blade-crossed emblem
of a family coat of arms, but with their lances
       hacked off. All they could emblazon now
is the sorry family Homo sapiens.

Ostraka

The eight winds blow,
an earthquake shakes Mount Olympus, cholera
ravages the states, drought everywhere, the mysterious
death of bees throughout the country,
the flowers and crops die, the hourly
slaughtering of innocents,
                        and all we do is debate
in the assembly, cast *ostraka*—shards of democracy—
regarding our ships, the color of their sails.

New Ostia

The red glow of the burning city towered into the sky.
The fetus of terror stirred in us. To witness people in flames
leap from windows, call out. Too much.
The old world brought down around our heads.
The aftermath a seething bewilderment.
Tribunes fan the sparks of public anxiety
into panic, dispatch soldiers to ports, stations,
set up roadblocks, search for weapons. Rumors
of another attack. Opposition cowed by accusations
of being soft, unpatriotic. Special measures called for.
A supreme commander set up
to combat threats, terrorist legions.
How a timorous population can be molded.
Powers ceded to our Pompey Magnus
and his cronies, lining their already lined pockets.

Another Empire

In notes to an old Greek poem, the Seleucid Empire is mentioned.
    An empire that was hot on the tongues of its denizens.
Whose fame spread thousands of leagues. Whom folk feared
    and bowed to. All hailed Emperor Hegorgebus,
who, according to the notes, was thought of in later times
    —in the cold horology of the universe, quicker than soon—
as a short-sighted, perverse numbskull under
    the thumb of every consul, praetor, general, and goon
in the agora, breaking the coffers, squandering revenue
    on the military while folk starved, the infirm left without care.
Still the demos went on glorifying him, their imperial buffoon.

Odysseus

I tried to finagle my way out of another
    manufactured military campaign, but what could I do
when that wiseacre, Palamedes, cast my son
    in the path of my plow team? The tears of my boy
on being manhandled, turned from fear
    to grief. I consoled Telemachus, said I'd not be gone long,
that he was boss for now. What I missed most on the windy plains
    of Troy amid the debacle, the death of friends,
the infamous voyage back, was my laughing boy
    with the big brown eyes, the pillow fights, the games
of tag, football, letting him pip me in the hoop race.
    When I did arrive back to my son, the man,
it was right that I should approach him disguised as a beggar.

Father Abroad

I avoid places where children play:
      squares where families congregate, parks
with swings, slides, monkey bars, seesaws;
      the seaside where yesterday I turned my head away
seeing a father and mother with their kid, the dad
      running, pretending not to be fast enough to catch up
with his laughing child. My Telemachus, my son,
      you tag me everywhere I go.

Life

When a god is against you it's bad enough,
      but when you're far from home, alone,
then fat chance. I found him gasping in surf,
      tended his wounds. I told my story, he his.
It's the intimacy of shared stories: the private
      woes of childhood, family, friends, daily battles
which strengthen the neuro-ties, the byssus
      securing lovers, as much as the body bonding.
I, of course, wanted him to stay, assured him
      it was natural to fret and yearn for his family.
We leaned on the portal of hope. When Hermes
      ordered me to let him go I obeyed for his sake,
helped build the raft. We wept. He yearned then
      to stay, wanting most what he couldn't have, daft
as any mortal. He had to go. Nothing else to know.

Parents

What do any of us know about our parents,
    separate or together? My mother kept the house
in order, prepared food, wore the *epinetron* smooth
    rolling the threads, the skeins of daily love.
She wove our clothes, played knucklebones, snakes & ladders,
    lined up with other women at the well,
walked home balancing the vase on her head
    as she balanced our family, the *oikos*.
Like most parents she hid her care, the arguments
    with my father heading off on another odyssey.
Da played dead when I stabbed him, let me
    wear his helmet; turned into a tickle monster.
Ma scolded him for exciting me before bed.
    I suppose they were like most parents. What do I know?
I had no others. They were mysterious as the night sky, the god
    hidden within the dark of the forbidden inner temple.

Go-Between

Forgive your fighting parents the post-argument silence game
assigning you go-between, their Hermes, till tension thawed:
"Tell your father dinner's ready," etc. Always the same.
Give thanks for making you their ankle-winged, fleet-as-thought god.

The Divorced Mother

Today you are Demeter, unable to eat, hair undone,
    holding a torch for your daughter. You go to the ends
of the earth for her, the earth itself in sympathy.
    You grieve not for half a year, but each half week
your child spends with Hades.
    And it isn't that your ex is that bad a guy,
it was just you found his company infernal
    in trivial ways, and not just when he forced his body
on you, revisiting that day you picked flowers in Enna.
    You harvest your free time,
sometimes yearn so much for your child that you long
    to be back in the place of asphodels,
dwell again in the security of family.

Humilities

You know the story. Zeus and Hermes came down
    to earth. No one took them in except an old couple.
Philemon set the table while Baucis
    prepared the meal: smoked bacon, vegetables
from their garden, feta and radishes, a dessert
    of apples and walnuts. The married pair realized
—noticing the amphora mysteriously brimmed after each pour—
    who was under their roof. What's not known is they begged
this brace of gods not to drown their inhospitable neighbors,
    not send the deluge. They outshone
the miffed deities then. Ah, the wisdom of old age,
    the humility to not care about one's own humility,
to be beyond the scruples of gods and mortals.

Goddess of the Hearth

And what about Hestia? We know little of her story.
    Where's the record of Penelope
and Telemachus playing checkers before the fire?
    Or the version in which Odysseus escaped the draft,
never left for Troy, enjoyed the solace
    of arriving home after work, pouring a glass of wine,
playing with his boy, having given thanks to the goddess?
    Hestia, as unassuming as many wives, husbands,
parents slaving at chores without a word
    of thanks, feeding the hearth, the embers rekindled.

Concealment

A man walked past. We practically
    brushed shoulders, the lane was so narrow.
I nodded, muttered a *kalimera,* but
    he chose to look ahead, ignore me.
I've seen that look, that demeanor before,
    always in rural towns, villages:
Toome, Morrisville, Derrynane, Delphi.
    Not simply the buttoned-up look that is the result
of living in a small community,
    but the face that stubbornly shuts out the invasion
of sightseers, yuppy realtors, outsiders.
    It conceals the gold bar of butter,
rancid or no, left buried in the bog,
    safe from any museum,
the last salted treasure of the lost world.

The Old Country

We are armed with cameras, guide books, maps;
      ready to grasp the spirit of the old world
that's like a slain emperor
      propped up on his saddle,
his horse whipped back into the battle's fray,
      convincing even his own side he's still alive.

The Green Line

Of all the roads, including the breathtaking cliff roads
      of Parnassus, the Healy Pass, or the drive over Coomakista,
the type of road we love most are those roadlings
      off the beaten track with grass breaking through
the tarred center, a green line: the one down to our house
      from the Pass of the Treasure, or the Serpentine Way,
a road you might see a yellow bunting, kingfisher, or badger.
      The grass is a sign, a grassroots demonstration
led by Gaia, or Dana declaring, "We shall overcome," or
      some such cliché. Daisies and dandelions shoot up
through asphalt, flowers stuck in the muzzles of guns.

Resort

       The ocean wraps its surf scarf round the shoulder
of the shore. Everything's in touch with everything else:
       the sky with the sea, the wave susurrus
with the zephyr in the fuchsia and furze, the cock crowing
       again and again, dawning on us
every second is now. And then the day trippers come,
       I among them, a scout,
already parked. The army of cars wind along the road.
       They glitter like the helmets of hoplites.
The legions take over for a while, then go,
       as is the way of all empires.

Foreigner

Good to be a stranger in a city, swan about
       its streets, lanes, quays, establish a headquarters
in a café or tavern, get to know the regulars
       but not long enough to see their other sides,
or be taken for granted. You, the fresh slate, the tabula rasa.
       Everyone seems so amiable. The character who wears
his cap at a rakish angle, the grumpy geezer with his young wife,
       the chatty woman who dresses in clothes too young for her.
Observe them tenderly: tipsy Pan, aging Aphrodite
       in short skirt, Zeus in from the rain,
his umbrella blown inside out, cursing "Boreas, that ass,"
       Leda giving you the eye—look out, trouble there.
Nothing like hobnobbing with the local pantheon.

The Mechanic

In a one-donkey town, Pyrgos, we drive to a garage
        glimpsed at the last T-junction, deflated as our tire.
In the doorway the mustached mechanic
        sits on a crate, as though waiting for us.
I point to the flat, indicate we've no spare.
        He jacks the car up, unscrews the bolts,
extracts the wheel damaged on the rim, hammers it
        good as new, mends the puncture,
bolts the tire back, all without a word
        between us and in less than five minutes.
Maybe this god of mechanics considers a puncture
        beneath his dignity. I'm inclined to think
he prefers his oily hands do the talking.
        He wipes them with a rag, grunts, turns away.

Heat Wave in Sitia

We take a break from the African heat under one of the palm trees
        with boles like giant pineapples that line the harbor.
The whitewashed houses scramble
        on each other's shoulders to catch sight
of the water, a ship on the horizon, bathers,
        fishing boats, the wavelets like fans
cooling the shore, the Attic woman in a black peasant shawl
        fanning her heat-wrinkled face. Her stoical daze
says we've seen many such days. We have survived.

The Third Voyage

Exhausted, we arrive in an out-of-the-way fishing town.
    The shabby hotel has the feel of a mariner's house.
Boats pass in the dark with their tilley lamps,
    and for a moment we think
that it is we who are on a moving boat
    as we watch the vessels motor out. In such a place
I fancy Odysseus planted his oar, tired of drifting.
    All he wanted was to be left alone, to settle
in such a foreign harbor, still
    have the illusion of being on water, of voyaging.
The best of both worlds, finding himself
    relieved of the demons of fame,
giving himself up to glorious anonymity.

Templenoe

The seine boats, colorful as jockeys, jockey each other
    at the starting line, with names like racehorses:
El Niño, Rainbow Warrior, The Liberator, Challenge,
    Golden Feather, The Kingdom. With a shot they're off.
The crowd lets out yelps, cheers subduing even
    the raffle seller, the ice cream van's jingle, the trinket stalls.
The gods of Tackiness, holy as they are, are beaten for now by local gods
    inciting each crew to win: the stocky helmsman of Waterville,
the shrewd Valentia man, the determined Derrynane one.
    The silver trophy glitters on Templenoe Pier,
winks that the gods of antiquity are with us still. Make no mistake
    about it. On Iveragh. Which one will lift the cup today?

Weather Relief

After days of unusually fine weather, a cloud
    settles like a hood on the peninsula, shuts out
this renowned ragged coastline:
    mythical islands, beaches, windy roads, tropical flora.
We're relieved of the sense nothing in us can
    match its unsettling splendor, that life
now is more clearly bearable,
    that we're more at home on a cloud-shrouded shore.

Good Company

The water washes up around a rock like a wind-blown
    wedding veil, a child's hand in a passing car waves
to a waving whitethorn bush, the turquoise of the sea near the shore
    and deeper teal far out are highlighted by the sun,
my smile reflects in your shades. Ah, nothing exists
    without another. It's good not to be alone, be alive even,
better anyway than yesterday, that gray mist
    like a drear god descended and made nothing
of everything. Nothing. But forget that now. Yesterday
    is defined only via today and today thankfully
via yesterday: everything made out of nothing rather
    than nothing made out of everything.

The Wall

A playful dog races his image
        on the tide-laminated sand.
The ocean itself is too turbulent
        to be a mirror. I'm more like the sea,
at least today, more a turbid empty storm
        repeatedly battering on
the eroded Rocks of Whyness.

The teacher testing catechism—the one
        that opened: *Who made the world?*—
was probably right. I irked him, raising my hand
        continually, attempting answers. I was always
too earnest. He pointed to the dunce's corner:
        "Face the wall, fool."

Sermon

> *. . . we have a savior who has been tempted in every way,*
> *just as we are—yet is without sin.*
> —HEBREWS 4:15

    These days the Savior could not come back to live
without sin among us, the matrix beneath the surface
    of daily existence being sewn so intricately
by that crafty angel, tireless Complicity.
    God's temples are heated by oil secured at the cost
of slaughter. The pillows He'd lie on are the feathers
    of the bird that saved Noah. Even a sackcloth would likely
have molecules of blood in its sweatshop stitches.
    He couldn't drop down, mosey
around town, take in His handy work: trees rising
    from concrete, the hubbub of folk about their workaday,
a passing woman who reminds Him of Magdalene, the smell
    of coffee. How He envies the creature
created in His own image. How He longs to become His image.
    How He pines for this earth. How absurd
the old God feels now. Our Image. Pray for Him.

The Apostle in Corinth

And so Paul proselytized in this place, the remains
        we stand upon below the limestone mountain,
Acrocorinth, with the hodgepodge fort
        harboring also the temple of Aphrodite,
the hotspot of call girls who satisfied local swanks.
        From here, he decried the ways of the flesh,
chastising those buckos for their profligate ways.
        What's not recorded is that he envied
their dedication to the flesh, shunning the thought
        that this was simply healthy fun. He fled,
not because he gave up on the Corinthians,
        but for fear he'd surrender to appalling desire.

Visiting the Church of Saint John of the Apocalypse, Patmos

Almost lunchtime. We enter the shining womb of the church
        with its solid gold candlesticks, tabernacle,
utensils, icons painted by anonymous priests
        portraying the Big End. All the caretaker cares about is
shepherding us out, tired of this holy show, this doomsdaying.
        The only prophecy he gives a damn about is the thought
of his welcoming mutt, light lunch, his ouzo, his divine siesta.

Sleep

We're hardly aware of Hypnos in all his guises.
        Consider the siesta, saving us from overbearing Helios,
mundane care, permitting us to catch up after a night
        nursing a sick child. And what about the catnap
on a train, or over a book in a library?
        We wake up, the battery recharged,
all set to burn midnight oil, dance, court, lift
        a glass with Dionysus. If we're sensible
we'll treat Hypnos properly, allow him his third of the day
        to treat our wounds, call in the Oneiroi,
the psychedelic boys, the dream makers to guide us
        through the magic mirrors, the surreal film
beneath our fluttering eyes, watching over our repose,
        before we shake ourselves free, face another day.

Our Times

When exactly we felt it we can't say, a tiredness beyond
        any we felt before, beyond age, beyond acedia,
beyond work, beyond burning the candle, beyond megrim
        and malinger. Our blood is mercury. We are heavy
as the cadaver of ourselves, lugging our own dead weight,
        a condensed black star, a tar-star
traveling night years, dropping uranium-dense tiredness,
        tiredness made night, sapping night.

Dawn

Waking, the sky clear, a few gray wisps
    of cloud in the firmament,
the only hint that the avuncular god of night
    was here, puffing away
on his clay pipe, all reverie I imagine,
    feet up, comfy, at ease
at last, watching over us, not wanting to wake us,
    his poor clay charges, too early, slipping off
on soft falling moccasins of light.

Birth Notice

This morning, mindlessly doing a marriage chore,
    making our bed, the smudge of your blood
on the white linen sheet wasn't the folklore
    seal of freshly opened womanhood,
but, rather, the branded red wax impression,
    sealing another month's quiet depression,
the privy stamp of childless parenthood.

Breakfast

Sip by sip Poseidon is away,
      the ebb tide draining the bay,
leaving cappuccino suds along the strand
      sprinkled with cinnamon of sand.

The Poetry World

Sunday morning, the train emerges not just from the tunnel
      of Penn Station, across from the catacombs,
the Palisades, the shining lordly Hudson, but from the hell
      of another excursion to hustle for my poems.
Enough. Head north to my hermitage.
      Know again the rapture of the pen across the page.

Lulu's Family Diner

I'm lucky enough to get a window seat
        overlooking the mountains, north of Adamsville Plain.
The landscape is a platinum blonde, dyed by fall.
        Lulu hums a country song, serves me home fries
the shade of the countryside. She tells me to make myself at home.
        Lulu is the beautiful muse of what they call homely.
I think I have a crush on her. She returns, asks
        if I want a refill. I tell her the home fries were the best
ever. This makes Lulu, lonely Lulu, lovely Lulu, happy.
        Not many can say they made a muse feel good.
Not many can say a muse called them "Honey."

To a Poet Friend

The door of our home is always open.
        Everyone knows the key is under the rock.
We never ask for thanks, being glad
        friends are there, finding a refuge.
Rancor rose in one seeing this house above the ocean,
        the islands named after gods, the lush wood,
garden, my happy wife and child stacking turf
        like gold bars against the side wall,
the cherry floors, wainscoting, books, some with my name
        on the cover: my life thus far that my poet-friend
leafed through, faulting me for all I'd done,
        or rather for all he hadn't, failure
by comparison. I said nothing. I wanted to tell him
        I feel I've achieved little also, but
to say this would have irked him all the more.
        He has thrown in the towel, left to be among those
who've given up. He's gone to join the failure club.

The Small Picture

The priest rambles on about how we're each a grain of sand
        —such a tiresome analogy. I almost blurted out
that he makes too much of us, that this grain is more like
        our star. Consider then the speck, too small
for the eye to see, our nanoling earth. Then imagine
        ourselves in the bigger picture. Yes,
I know the story, but today your few words of praise
        —what does it matter what you praised?—
made me forget my smallness. Puffed me up,
        comedic as it sounds. Who knows, it may
be true. Who knows, we all may be worthwhile. Imagine.

Dropping Names

To go unnoticed is good, though mostly we forget
        and silently crave attention, fame,
to be seen, adored even, above all others.
        Listen to rain's patter on your hut
away from everyone. If you have any need to drop a name
        then rub elbows, hobnob with the likes of demigod Solitude
or the irenic deity of the rain, an unseen local god
        whose name's long forgotten, or unknown.

Arion's Retribution

On the voyage home the other sailors coveted his poetry prize. As they were about to kill him, his song drew dolphins to the ship that bore him to safety in Taenarum.

His best days were there on Taenarum, startled
    to be still alive, finding his bearings,
kneeling in the morning grass embrocated with dew,
    wondering at the lambent eyes
of creatures at night, the nervy rustle of animals
    in the woods, the lizards lolling
under the sun, the general pellucid light
    sparking on the quartz rock, Apollo's encomium.
He knew then the contiguity of all his eyes fell on
    during his exile, when folk took him
for dead. This was his halcyon time, turning misfortune
    into felicity, such a crucial survival skill.
                                  But it was not
until recuperated, in need of company
    and on the road back to Corinth that he realized this boon.
Arriving in the capital, not without regret
    and reservation, he told his story to the court.
Though in this variant—for this has happened before
    and to other Arions—he bade Periander to stay his hand
when the ship of laureled fellow sailors
    strutted into town thinking they were home
and dry. He said, "Perianth, do not condemn them to Hades,
    rather allow me to stand before them on the proscenium
and lavish gratitude with my song hoard, for it was only
    by virtue of their foul play that I was blessed with this
word-booty on the bounteous isle of Taenarum."

To Those in the Shade

Let us speak of the partners, wives, husbands
        and children of the limelit ones.
Penelope rather than Odysseus, the wives
        of the gallivanting apostles, their daughters and sons
left behind or dragged all over Galilee,
        the forgotten husband of Lesbia
to whom she dedicated poems long since lost.
        Or Arion's wife who cooked his meals,
washed his clothes, made sandwiches
        as he set off on another reading tour.
She put up with his tantrums, his bouts
        of writing under the spell of a new muse,
his petty jealousies in the literary arena,
        poets jockeying to ride Pegasus into the ground.
Praise all those in the shade of the limelight.

The Era of Busy

The drudgeries of another day ticked off the list,
        the palimpsest already filling with tomorrow's chores.
We barely keep our snorkel above the relentless waves
        of busy-ness in an era in which, according to the soothsayers
of our childhood, we'd be awash with oceans of time,
        what with computers, mechanization.
But my first chance to catch a breather
        —allowing me a quick read of short poems, and
jot this on the back of tomorrow's list—is waiting in a bar
        for a friend who thankfully is late. I call for a beer.
The muses, with such little time to ambush, must strike swiftly.
        They're the resistance, the partisans from Helicon. The foam
of a few moments to myself overflows the frosted glass.

Master Tardy

Late again. Another train missed. The doors shut in your face.
      You leave everything to the last second; never one
to waste time waiting, you waste it even more consigned
      to the waiting room. Vexation and frustration turn
to acedia. The Spirit of Punctuality is out to teach you a lesson.
      Even kings are sentenced to schedules, timetables.
You're under the thumb of tyrant Tardy. He'll be the death
      of you. All you'll be early for is your own funeral.

"The Good Die Young"

The guy who uttered this first winced that his remark
      had become a maxim. He complained that he blurted
this hogwash to parents whose daughter drowned herself,
      that his consolation sprang from being at a loss
for words. He thought better of all the souls
      who fumble through to middle age, worn down
by the path alternating mostly between rocky way
      and sinking mulch; bonds and hopes that seemed infrangible
sagging like torn twigs, leaves at half mast, snapped stems;
      the branch-backlash of a lover or friend as they forge ahead;
will inclining to velleity, exhaustion even in the vales
      of joy or the brief clearings of the day.
You, who have left the groves of youth,
      struggle through the muddy, tangled wood of middle age,
the dense gnarled forest of the elder,
      laud yourselves now, the good who muddle on.

Understory

Redwood sorrel is so adapted to dim light
      that its heart-shaped leaf
folds down and hides under direct sunshine,
      opens up in shade, diffused rays. We're not
unlike that plant, never getting far from earth,
      hardly able to take the fierce light of joy,
or bliss, nor the pitch night
      of despair or fear. We survive best
in the shadows, the understory of our days.

About Time

Today I want to thank the daily god of unhappiness,
      petty worries, disgruntlements, sorrows great
and small, for having taken such good care of me,
      making himself at home in my days,
and for taking the odd break as now he slips away
      into the background, smiling kindly,
delivering me into the care of his shy sibling, Peace,
      at traffic lights on Pearl and Union as the sun
softens the snow-bunkered street, the ice-cased lake.
      We turn into our clearer selves like snow and rime
turn to water. I wave a driver ahead. He avidly
      waves thanks. I would like to wave
gratitude to the god of unhappiness.
      He could've finished me off often enough.
His present absence accentuates my happytime.

Special Days

Give us the regular day any day, not
one hyped up, brimming with expectation:
a wedding, bank holiday, birthday, Christmas.
We *must* enjoy the gifts, new clothes, family.
The tyranny that we should be grateful
for the bounty of victuals, flavored by
sauce-thoughts of those starving elsewhere.
Spare us such a day bloated with despair.

In Praise of Failure

Make no mistake, it's good to get the thumbs down,
    not subject to the crowd's praise, knowing most
take their cue from the heads of the day.
    Besides we've got this upside down. That actually thumbs
down directed the winner to stick his sword in the ground, to *not*
    take the loser's life. I was fortunate to see the royal thumb
point earthward, to slip away, wounded, spurned, but still alive,
    released from the arena, free of responsibility,
to be myself, favored by the emperor of obscurity.

A Selection from the Athenian Workshop Papyrus

The following four poems are from an exercise given by Gregory the Elder in the Athenian Workshop after the participants' night at a local symposium.

I
Aubade

I didn't resort to the hair of the god
    that bit me. Being by the sea I went for a dip.
Afterwards I never felt better,
    my hangover dispelled by the trident deity,
the cold brine shocking the system out of its doldrums,
    soothing it, lifting it like a wave,
sparkling in the sun. Poseidon is a swell.
    Now I'm myself again it's time to celebrate,
to raise a cup to you, Dionysus. Cheers. Your health.

II
PASU
(Post-Alcoholic Sexual Urge)

This morning I woke at dawn—cock crow
    would be more correct, Chrysilla, after all
the vino yesterday. Wouldn't you know,
    you had no mind for a morning call,
my drinker's alarm clock, nudging you awake.
    And last night—my hot wife—
you were in the thrall of Himeros. But for Bacchus's sake,
    I had the wine-decline. Oh, drooping life.

III
Cycles

Usually after periods of solitude, domesticity, work,
        I'm swept by the sense that something's missing,
another Antaeus touching down
        on the ground of the earthy, the flesh of night
to be reminded that life is tastier
        seasoned by the salt of anxiety, the pepper of guilt.

IV
The Artist's Disgrace

The player strums, tires of what he loves
        to do, plays from the graveyard of his self
for a few drachmas. Local muses revive him.
        Let not the music of this place
suffer such disgrace, the bouzouki itself pregnant
        on its back, patiently waiting to give birth.

The Most Neglected God of All

Now let us praise the most neglected god of all,
    the god of the Hand Job, Hand Shandy, Master
Spank the Monkey, Madame Frig. The god
    that everyone: housewives, presidents,
gurus, zen monks—so that's the One Hand Clap—rabbis, nuns
    are possessed by, ever since it was handed down
to Pan who in turn handed it on to shepherds. The god Atum,
    who the Egyptians say gave rise to us all.
Not The Big Bang then, but The Big Hand Job. The god
    who pouts that we never pay him public due.
We're ashamed, embarrassed at having lit
    a furtive candle to him. Myriads down
through the ages have attended his daily secret service
    wherever the members of his church could find:
offices, buses, alleys, bathrooms, beaches, cars.
    There's hardly a spot on earth
people haven't laid their offering. What's the strangest place
    you've communed with this handy god? Even as we speak
millions of hands are busy all over the world.
    You yourself may have been blessed by him today.
Have you given thanks? Enough of turning a blind eye,
    of being small, stunted. Come now.

The Ladykiller

Suddenly, catching myself in the mirror,
    —hard to figure what precipitated this shift,
appropriately in the Old Town Bar—the timeless self-image
    of a curly, handsome twenty-something-year-old
fell away before my eyes and I saw this unfamiliar
    gray-haired chap, hair receding above his temple.
Only this morning the world was at my feet, God's gift
    to women, a ladykiller. The Graiae, three crones
born white-haired, nudge each other on nearby stools.
    My new girlfriends flirt with me, only one tooth
between them in their snickering heads.

The Goat

When you reach to help the hurt creature
    it usually reacts in fear
—what does it know of goodwill? Remember
    that day on Coomakista Pass
the goat that had trapped its head
    in a wire box fence. No matter
from what angle we patiently approached
    it bucked,
the wire cutting into its neck all the more
    till finally we gave up. The memory
of that goat haunts me, I
    being in the grip of old ways,
old goat ways I never
    seem to slip free of, helpless
to untangle goathead himself, desperate
    to hold to that one security.
At least this he knows. At least this
    is certain.

Tug-of-War

Right now the old conventional tug-of-war goes on.
        The Pheromones versus the Choice team.
The thigh muscles bulge, faces strain puce.
        The sweaty heroic battle.
Exhausting. The best we can expect is
        the Choice side holds, and not allow
the other side—Boozing Bill, Delia Dope,
        Dusty Lust & Co.—to drag them, the underdogs,
over the line till they lie beaten, grimacing in the dirt,
        the Pheromones doing a lap of honor, brandishing
the cup, cheering, gloating through every cell of the body.

Addict

I'm like those dolphins
        I read about, confined in isolated cells
              of a pool with sliding doors.
A zoologist manipulated their encounters,
        observing their sexual behavior.
The one released dolphin
        refusing to take afterwards to the sea,
              head-butting the pool's gate to get back in.

On Miami Beach

A blind couple, hand in hand, tap their way along the boardwalk.
    Hardbodies laid out on the beach, the golden altar
of the body-beautiful, check each other out.
    Look at that shining Adonis, this bikini-clad Helen.
It isn't wise to test the gods, be granted what is wished for,
    but now I envy this couple, their unseeing sight.
Neither one is a looker. What does that matter? They see better
    in their way, free of the look in vogue,
that tanned body, those muscular thighs, that hourglass figure
    telling time, the skin-shallow despot focusing the eye.

Escaping the Party

Our eyes meet and hold. The alcohol is a potion,
    freeing inhibitions. We forget we're married
but not to each other. We escape to an out-of-the-way bar.
    Kissing, our tongues flicker
in and out of one another, flames of votive candles
    at a saint's dark side-altar, praying for a miracle,
released from concern, responsibility.
    The wax of intermingling candles
weeps below the beatific, sorrowful face,
    the merciful patron saint of adulterers.

From the Acropolis View Hotel

Hephaestus tried to ravish Athena, but she fled and his
seed spilled on the Acropolis.

This afternoon you were Athena on the balcony
        in a short black dress, commando style,
your open tanned thighs revealing the only shrine
        I kneel to lately. But today my adoration, my come-on
was repelled. You weren't in the mood.
        I was the deformed god making my advances.
But this time you showed a modicum of sympathy, Athena,
        letting down your shoulder strap, raising your dress a tad.
A flashing goddess. I, Hephaestus, spurted on
        the ground below the Parthenon, a relieved voyeur.

Return

Unable to stop ourselves, we parked off the road in Arcadia,
        clambered down into the copse. Everyone is overcome
by the gods from time to time, possessed by them, like it or no.
        I was Pan, goatee and all. You were Syrinx,
but this time you didn't make a bolt for it,
        didn't turn yourself into a reed.
We made out in that bug-infested sacred grove,
        assisted by last night's Viagra.
We managed to ignore the pestering insects,
        the traffic flashing by on the road to Sparta.

"Try Again, Dolt"

We spiced up the lust of our living dust
    watching ourselves in the mirror's blue movie,
pistoning . . . Forgive us, Eros, our failure,
    who simply want sullied words to praise you,
releasing us from the quotidian: our workaday,
    the prolonged winter, the snow
falling outside as though you yourself tore up
    this page and cast it into the air,
saying, "Try again, dolt, to praise the act,
    the glory of the friction of the bodies sparking off
each other like chips of flint, blazing up
    in the winter wilderness, in the ancient way."

Mercy

The attractants raced like a riotous mob, usurping self-rule,
    the congress of flesh through partly open clothes.
We were beyond caring if the waitress noticed
    two flushed people entering the restroom.
Afterwards the Erotes relinquish control,
    take a breather as we order coffee. You bury
your head back in your book and I in mine,
    as if nothing happened, and twenty years pass
and I mutter something about how awful
    to be at the mercy of the flesh, that frenzied groping.
Oh, my long-legged goddess of the loo.

Purgatory

I want you to tell me everything will be hunky-dory,
        perfect, not unlike the way I wanted the priests' stories
of Heaven to be true. Hell and Purgatory
        are more believable. There are no guarantees.
To ask for heaven is to make a hell of Purgatory.

Payment

Great, the time-out of lovemaking, no
        doubt about that. I was lucky
to have experienced the body of Aphrodite
        —wearing merely a silky thong. But
there's payment for such good fortune.
        Sadness, Loneliness, Longing are like vultures
hovering over the god, Ecstasy, waiting to descend
        and pick the bones of the Eros
even at the very first, tender shut-eyed kiss.

Avaunt

And since we have separated for better
        and for worse I'm in withdrawal
from love's heroin shot, tended by the downer gods
        congratulating each other, having plucked
our lovebug wings. They're like kids who rip the wings
        off butterflies, gleefully watch them flop in a jam jar.
I'll not go on, not give that bunch the satisfaction
        of garlanding our misfortune as they bid the muse
of tragedy herself, Melpomene, to my side. Enough, avaunt.
        I feel just fine, sweet, cool, Sir Cheerful himself.

The Rat

Bad enough to miss you, but to think of you
        with another. It's as though a rat,
sensing he's about to gnaw his way out of my chest,
        intensifies his efforts behind
my rib cage, tissue, muscle. Any minute now
        his smirking, whiskered chin will rip
through my flesh, appear with my pulsating heart
        in his dripping fangs.

"It's an Ill Wind That Blows No Good"

But the reverse is true too.
      A good wind often blows some ill.
You were the good wind that blew
      the daily missing you. The wind blows still.

The Break-up Contract

Who'd have thought we'd come to this a year ago?
      I sang happy birthday, a mite tipsy, over the phone.
I gave you gypsy earrings, chiffon scarves, a lapis ring. We were so
      sure of our future together. Now you're on your own.
Now I'm on my own. My present to you on this day
      is not to make contact with you in any way.

Meeting Again

A wound itches as it heals.
        Scratching will reopen the cut.
We met once more. Of course
        the wound bled.
Festered afterwards. But what
        a relief to let ourselves go, to tear
and tear at that love scab.

Later

I sit in the same square, in the same overpriced café,
        watch the same frantic stream
of people pass by, the same comic pigeons
        reminding me of the way everyone speed-walks
in silent movies. I browse my book, come across
        a poem with that familiar quote of Heraclitus,
that nobody steps in the same stream twice.
        You stepped here only a week ago.

Old Flame

From Riverside Drive a cloud wraps the distant mountain summit
      in a mohair scarf, the type a woman might drape about her neck,
a female who jams words in my Adam's apple.
      The traffic is bottlenecked. The lights turn
from red to green and back to red. Too late.
      I notice my gray hair in the rearview mirror.
A woman strolls through my reflection. She is the image of one
      I vowed to spend my life with once. The traffic begins to flow.
No going back now. Gone forever, sipping her take-away coffee,
      her ambrosia this bitter morning. Oh, my cold old muse,
old flame. Daughter of Mnemosyne, cruel you are today.

A Quiet Glory

You must hold on after all these years
      of natter about sport, pulchritude, family, work,
the state of the world. The repetition of wilting stories.
      When all else fails—Eros, family, work—
it has been faithful; supportive on bad days
      like the trellis set in the earth so that hardy climbers,
glories, can wind their way up. Without friendship,
      maybe the greatest of all glories, you'll not fully bloom.

Worth Remembering

The only army of the ruined Acropolis of Sparta now
        is the army of ants filing back and forth over the stoa, the barracks,
the soldiers' mess hall, the sanctuary of Artemis Orthia
        where whipping contests to toughen young boys were held.
Time isn't that bad after all. Sure, all good things
        come to an end, but all dreadful things come to an end also.

The Caryatids in the Acropolis

So when the ruling, puffed-up males
        boast this is Democracy's birthplace,
let them consider us, the silent stone females,
        faces erased, holding up the roof-beams of our race.

The New Athena

If the gods are simply players within mortals
      then it's time to lay down my armor, plumed helmet, spear,
the aegis of my goat-skinned shield with gorgon's head.
      I pit difference between peoples: the Egyptians, Turks,
Trojans, the States, igniting their battle cry,
      the gore glory of war. Now I must allow my wise side
to emerge and break the cycle. I'll have a word
      in the ear of Ares, my blood-thirsty brother.
Even he's weary. I must now be solely the deity
      within you who seeks a resolution
without bloodshed, guardian of the few who command
      with their stentorian voice: "No more."

Laughter

On Centre Street, Skala, fuming with traffic,
      tired-faced mothers wheel prams, a procession
of schoolchildren wave flags,
      commemorating another military victory
—Ares smiling smugly on his infants.
      Three old women chat nine to a baker's dozen
outside the laundromat. I haven't a clue about what
      they say, but it's mirthful. The woman
without spectacles breaks
      into laughter, bends over in stitches
with a heartiness I haven't heard for ages
      at whatever the others say.
They've taken everything from life, wear black
      for all the reasons women wear black.
They've outshone even their own god,
      the orthodox God that never laughed.
May the memory of these women, the three graces,
      be with me now and in the hours of our darkness.

Disarming

A middle-aged woman—plain you might say—strolls by
    our house. I was out of sorts, not long up,
but her serene smile, without saying a word,
    remarks: "Take in the sun on the lake,
the honeysuckle's pink fingers bursting into yellow flames,
    the traffic on North Avenue for once gone so quiet
you can hear the whir of the hummingbird's wings
    reversing in midair." On another morning such serenity
would have vexed me, but there is something so natural
    about her demeanor. She doesn't notice me.
Disarmed, I let what bothers me go
    and think since there's no corresponding god
—the pantheon being all tiresome piss and vinegar—
    we must create a new order and call her
Tranquilia, Calmes, or promote Halcyon and tell Aphrodite,
    Ares, Artemis, even Zeus, to move over in the pecking order,
set her smack in the middle, the woman
    who breezes by our house this divine morning.

Patient

The snow has melted clean off the mountain.
        It's winter still. Yet another indication that Gaia
is in trouble, that things aren't sound.
        The rocky mountain top shines
like the bald head of a woman after chemo
        who wills herself out of her hospital bed
to take in the trees, the squirrels, the commotion
        in town, sip beer in a dive, smile
at the child ogling her shiny head, wishing
        it didn't take all this dying to love life.

Speaking Plainly

So few care in comparison to the many
        that it might as well be no one.
The sun glaring through the Cyclops' eye
        of the atmosphere wipes out frogs,
whips up hurricanes, melts behemoth bergs.
        Forget that spin of how even one person
or creature can alter the world,
        that a butterfly flapping its wings
or a leaping toad can set off a wonder-chain.
        For myriads now, too late.

Fathoming

Our child, our sprat, gazes across the sea, unable to fathom
        the teeming life beneath: cod, eel, shark, porpoise,
the clownish cuckoo wrasse that I never imagined
        could exist till hauling lobster off Scariff Island.
This iridescent creature, no more than five inches long,
        dazzled in the cage of the wire pot.
Our tiller man dryly remarked, "Ah, that's
        just a wee cuckoo wrasse. Worthless."
I knew I could never catch the rainbow wonder
        writhing there on the deck, a creature instantly
losing neon hues in this fishy upper world, dying under
        our scaled eyes. Ah, forgive us, wee cuckoo wrasse.

Well You Know This Fish

False cleanerfish mimic harmless cleaner wrasse:
        larger fish stop by for a routine wash;
a seeming symbiotic lick; the false fish
        tears into shocked flesh—what brass.

The New Pastoralists

Good it is to get off the beaten track, to chance upon
      an untrodden realm: the mall of trees, fluttering pennants
of leaves and butterflies, wildflowers, the creek. Arcadia.
      The dragonflies are stretch-limos chauffeuring spirits
of the natural world through the portals of our senses.
      The muse of the pastoral steps down the waterfalls
in a dashing white gown. She requests makers
      to burst forth into idylls lauding her once more, especially
now we mortally hurt her. The trees and water applaud.

The Other

Time to raise a paean to the carrion flies, olive-green slugs,
mauve maggots, slime-emerald algae, dandruff-creamy worms;
to all who make nothing of the corpse. The skin-crawling bugs
we turn our heads away from, the loathsome swarms,
the steaming dung dolloped on the soil that springs roses,
potatoes, tomatoes, the food on our tables. Doff our hats
to all the matter and mites we look down our snotty noses
upon. Admit that we are blind, hoodwinked, dumb, bats
—praise the bats too—that we are the great ungrateful.
Give thanks, erect monuments to them, the other beautiful.

The Winner

The bluebottle reigns supreme now
        over the kingdom of a carcass—
it doesn't matter to the fly if it's a cow,
        rat, swan, salmon, human, or ass.
The bluebottle is a glimmering gem
        not on Death's, but on Life's diadem.

Old-Timers

One fat geezer stretches his stone-studded, dewlapped neck
        toward the opposite bank of the Miami River:
the Jade Building, the Ambassadors, the Four Seasons,
        the Bank of America. The iguanas have come to Florida
to retire also. They have seen so many creatures, epochs come
        and go. These little dinosaurs take in rays
like the movie idols in a five-star hotel
        less than a hundred yards away. The stars baste slowly,
tanning around the pool, favored by the god of fame,
        the human need to create gods, bring gods down
to earth. The iguanas smirk from ear to ear.

Life

The taste of drink: the subtle tang of white wine,
> the bitter slug of stout, the burning nip of brandy,
the sour cut of beer, swigged, quaffed, and sipped: life
> distilled or fermented, hitting the spot
with a taste of more, leaving an aftertaste,
> a tantalizing sense of the perfect.

Another Time

A man plays a squeeze box in a pub that's one of the old types,
> lyceum of another time.
He braille-buttons the melodeon, squeezes life back
> into a worn tune. People jaw away around the bar,
pay no heed to this avatar, the air necromanced into music.
> Not even the player knows how good he is.
The tragedy now is not so much that nobody notices
> a god, but that even the gods don't know they are gods.

Wonder of Wonders

A girl cries. Her father beats her, convinces her she's dumb.
        She'll land back in that cave of herself again and
again for the rest of her life. Many are like mythical characters
        blindly returning to tackle whatever invisible monsters
brought them down long ago. Maybe the wonder
        of wonders of being alive—greater even than the lake
like a glittering shield, the leaves turning tangerine,
        bronze, ruby and so infinitely on—is, as yet,
we have not undone our world,
        and should we each manage to wrestle
our own special Trauma to the ground, tame him,
        there is Thanatos—his natural father—waiting
at the end of it all, the bigwig behind all the trouble.
        Time to give ourselves a pat on the back,
thumbs up, for not having blown ourselves sky-high.

News in Flight

We fly over the city. The screen flashes current news.
        Nothing, it seems, but killing and mayhem.
Daily we're brought low, how far we've fallen.
        Hardly anyone says a word. Urban lights stretch into
the rural night below. Even fewer mention such wonders.
        The lights are like those of fans at a concert
holding up candles to their god, Homo sapiens,
        fleeting as any. Yet gods nonetheless,
bearing mayhem on the one hand and marvels
        on the other, as is the way of any band of gods.

Time Travel

The train emerging out of the tunnel
       underneath the Acropolis, zooms through the agora
right by the Stoa of Attalos, the temple of Ares,
       the Panathenaic Way, Zeus's joint,
the very ground Plato frequented, where Socrates was imprisoned,
       where Aristophanes pulled the leg
of Demosthenes, Euripides plotted his soap operas. Look here,
       the subway train emerges out of the underworld of the future.

The Traveler's Grace

Nothing like landing in a foreign city
       early morning. Preferably in weekday hubbub.
Everyone going about their business, lost in themselves,
       not a thought of how strange, foreign, alien their lives are.
How abnormal to think it normal to find ourselves
       on a spinning ball reeling around a star
at thousands of miles per hour from who knows where
       to who knows where. How outlandish.
I'm one of the sacred dead,
       released from the underworld
of the mundane, the banal. Behold the normal.

DEDICATIONS AND ACKNOWLEDGMENTS

The following poems are dedicated in this way:
"Chronicle": for Jimnasius;
"To a Teacher": for Iono the Dramatist;
"Humilities": for Anna;
"The Third Voyage": for Bobysseus Dyladi;
"The Small Picture" to Heanius and Christophorus Silentiarius;
"Avaunt": for Elina Makropulos;
"A Quiet Glory": to Davus the Consul and Antonel of Carrucius.

Many of these poems previously appeared in the Academy of American Poetry's "Daily Poem" series; *Agenda; Alaska Quarterly Review; Alhambra Poetry Calendar 2009; Archipelago; Atlantic Monthly; Battersea Review; Daedalus; Dark Matter; Financial Times; Fulcrum; Green Mountains Review; Irish Times; Literary Imagination; New Ohio Review; Oxford Poetry; PN Review; Poetry Ireland Review; Poetry London; Poetry Review; Raintown Review; Riddle Fence; So Little Time; Southward;* the *Sunday Times* (UK), the *Times Literary Supplement*; and *Tuesday.*

Poems also appeared in *Best of Irish Poetry 2007; Best of Irish Poetry 2008; Love Poet, Carpenter: Michael Longley at Seventy,* ed. Robin Robertson; and *That Island Never Found: Essays and Poems for Terence Brown.*

A small number of the poems were included in two other of my books: *The New Citizen Army* (2010), published by the Combat Paper Project, and *Loosestrife* (2011), published by Fomite Press.

I would like to acknowledge the John Simon Guggenheim Memorial Foundation for a Guggenheim Poetry Fellowship, which allowed me the time to write a number of the poems, and Saint Michael's College. I would like to thank David Curzon, Gail Holst-Warhaft, Christopher

Ricks, Nicholas Rynearson, Judith Wilson, and all those who helped me to finalize this book. I also want to remember and acknowledge Katherine Washburn, who originally put me on to *The Greek Anthology* not long before she unexpectedly died.

Finally, I am grateful for a stay of some months in Centre Culturel Irlandais, Paris, while writing this book.

www.ingramcontent.com/pod-product-compliance
Lightning Source LLC
Chambersburg PA
CBHW030122170426
43198CB00009B/702